Warkworth Castle and Hermitage

John Goodall

Introduction

Warkworth Castle and Hermitage form one of the most spectacular pairings of medieval monuments in Britain. The castle straddles the neck of a naturally defensible spur of land created by a tight loop in the River Coquet, protecting the town of Warkworth and dominating the surrounding landscape. The castle was probably laid out in its present form by Roger fitz Roger in about 1200 and was developed by its subsequent owners, the Percy family, the earls (and later dukes) of Northumberland. The scale and ambition of this great building embody the power and pretensions of this noble family, among the greatest landowners in northern England. Less than a mile distant, tucked away on the banks of the River Coquet upstream and accessible only by boat, are the picturesque remains of a rock-cut chapel known as the hermitage, probably established in about 1400.

The castle at Warkworth has developed around two principal landscape elements: a high, artificial mound, called a motte, and a bailey, or fortified enclosure. On top of the motte lies the great tower, built after 1377 by the first Percy earl of Northumberland. It fell into ruin only in the 17th century, later than other parts of the castle. The bailey buildings beneath are the result of more than 400 years of architectural development, from the 12th to the 16th centuries. In their present condition, they bear the stamp of a massive reordering of the castle undertaken in about 1480 by the fourth earl of Northumberland, whose ambitious residence absorbed many older buildings.

Above: Henry Percy, first earl of Northumberland, takes an oath of loyalty to Richard II, in a detail from a 14th-century manuscript. The earl later played an active role in putting Henry IV on the English throne in Richard's place

Facing page: The great tower of the castle seen from the west, standing high on the motte

The Tour

The motte-and-bailey castle and first stone buildings at Warkworth probably date from about 1200. In the late 14th century, Henry Percy, first earl of Northumberland, built the magnificent great tower to symbolise his power.

FOLLOWING THE TOUR

Starting at the Lion Tower, on the left of the bailey, the tour takes in the bailey buildings before exploring the great tower. It continues (by ferry) to the hermitage. The numbers beside the headings highlight key points on the tour and correspond with the small numbered plans in the margins.

▮ LION TOWER

The Lion Tower, on the left of the castle bailey diagonally opposite the ticket office, was built as the main porch to the new bailey residence created by the fourth earl of Northumberland in about 1480. Its spectacular display of heraldic sculpture celebrated his dynastic prowess. Symbolic of the Percy family is the great lion over the door. Above this are two shields, each one formerly surmounted by a battle helm with a 'cap of estate' and a crest, respectively expressing the rank and identity of the wearer. Around the helms are representations of mantling, or decorative swathes of cloth. One of the badges at the top of the tower has tentatively been identified as the padlock or fetterlock of the House of York. If so, this would date the porch to before the Tudor victory at the Battle of Bosworth in 1485.

The vaulted ground floor led into the great hall. The stone wall benches here could have been used by waiting visitors. A door to the right led towards the incomplete collegiate church and a spiral stair, which gave access to the upper floors of the tower and the lost range next to it.

Facing page: The great tower seen from the south. The masonry and detailing of this 14th-century building are of the highest quality

THE LION TOWER

▮ The Percy lion. Its collar displays the family war-cry, 'Esperaunce', meaning 'hope'

2 The arms of Percy 'ancient', abandoned by the family in 1343, when the seal bearing these arms was smashed at Warkworth (see page 36)

3 The three 'luces', or fishes, of the arms of the Lucy family are a play on their name. The Percys inherited substantial estates from the Lucys in the 1380s

4 Family badges visible here are (from the left): the padlock or fetterlock of the House of York; the Percy crescent; and the portcullis of the Herbert family, into which the fourth earl of Northumberland married in 1472

5 The details of this fan vault relate the porch to the splendid 15th-century nave screen of York Minster

The Percy Household

A rich and powerful
medieval nobleman
needed the support
of a host of followers,
from minstrels to priests

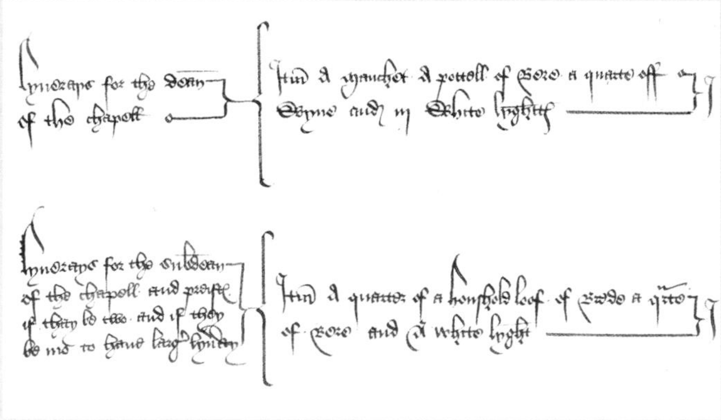

[handwritten manuscript extract]

*Above: An extract from the
Northumberland Household Book
relating to liveries, or doles of food,
drink and candles*
*Below: Musicians playing the drum,
harp and other instruments in a
16th-century manuscript illustration.
The fifth earl of Northumberland's
household included minstrels, singers,
choristers and an organist*

A great household in the late Middle Ages was a complex
organisation, employing people from every walk of life in the
service of a single, powerful individual. The workings and scale
of the Percy household are illustrated in the household records
and regulations brought together in two large volumes for the
fifth earl of Northumberland in about 1512. These are known as
the Northumberland Household Book. Although the earl lived
mainly in Yorkshire, the regulations reflect what life would have
been like at Warkworth when he visited the castle.

There were 166 permanent members of the fifth earl's
household, including 10 clerks to run his administration,
2 cupbearers, 2 carvers, a painter, a joiner, 2 falconers, 20 grooms,
6 child servants and 3 minstrels, who played the tabor, lute and
rebec. Serving his chapel were a dean, 6 chaplains (one of whom
was required to write dramatic entertainments called interludes),
8 gentlemen singers, 6 choristers and an organist. When the earl
travelled, he took with him a smaller 'riding household' of 57 men.
Such a group might have occupied the great tower at Warkworth.
As was typical in this period, the household was almost
exclusively male.

Daily life was governed by a strict timetable. The two
principal meals of the day, at 10am and 4pm, were eaten with
much ceremony. Waiting on such a powerful man was not
considered a menial occupation. The earl, his wife and his heir
were served at table by ten servants, who included his two
youngest sons. The household officers worked in shifts. Twenty
gentlemen, yeomen officers and grooms waited on the earl in
the great chamber between 6am and noon. Their number
increased to 30 in the evening.

The Northumberland Household Book also reveals the
entertainments laid on for special occasions: a performance by
the king's jugglers, visits during the feast of St Nicholas of the
boys appointed for the day as bishops of York and Beverley, and,
on New Year's Eve, a Nativity play by members of the chapel.

2 HALL RANGE

Extending across the west side of the bailey was the hall range, entered through the Lion Tower. On the left were the great hall and the formal withdrawing chambers. To the right lay the service rooms, entered through a cluster of three doors in the end wall of the great hall. Only the stubs of two of these doors and the fragmentary foundations of the chambers to which they led now remain.

Immediately next to the great hall were the pantry, where bread was kept, and the buttery, for storing and serving beer. The kitchen was reached down a corridor between the buttery and pantry and was separated from the hall by a small yard, to prevent the spread of cooking fires. The kitchen, which was laid out on a square plan, had two large fireplaces. One of these retains its dripping pan: the juices for basting meat were collected in the stone drain on the ground and ran into a pot. Against the curtain wall is a drain and beside this a stone water trough, worn by the scooping of buckets. Tiny fixing marks in the wall above the trough suggest that the water was supplied from a lead tank. Beside the kitchen are the remains of a larder.

Just beyond the kitchen is a side gate tower, or postern, built in about 1200, through which food was probably delivered. Its upper floors were adapted as accommodation in the late Middle Ages. An inventory made about 1574 notes a falconer's chamber and hawks' mew in this area of the castle.

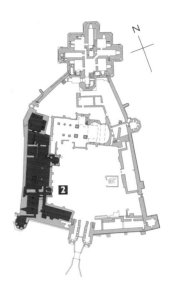

Below: A view of the hall range from the east. On the right are the postern gate and the ruins of the kitchen and services. To the left of the Lion Tower are the remains of the great hall and Little Stair Tower

RECONSTRUCTION OF THE LATE FIFTEENTH-CENTURY HALL RANGE

1 Lion Tower – the porch and main entrance

2 Arcade in the great hall

3 Central hearth

4 Dais and high table

5 Little Stair Tower

6 Privy entrance to withdrawing rooms

7 Stair and lobby to great chamber

8 Chapel

9 Chapel closet

10 Carrickfergus Tower

11 Buttery and pantry with chambers over

12 Louvre or smoke vent

Above: A reconstruction of the hall range as rebuilt in about 1480 by the
fourth earl of Northumberland. The new building made extensive use of
earlier structures, and provided a set of domestic chambers and service
rooms that mirrored the arrangements in the great tower

*Right: A king dining in state,
in an early 15th-century French
manuscript illumination. The table
is set across the width of the room,
as the earl of Northumberland's
table would have been in the great
hall at Warkworth*

▤ GREAT HALL

The great hall created by the fourth earl in the late 15th
century was essentially a remodelling of an earlier hall built
against the curtain wall in about 1200. The older building
incorporated a stone bench against the curtain wall and was
divided lengthwise into two aisles of unequal width by an
arcade of three stone arches – a fairly typical arrangement for
the period. Two bases for the arch columns survive, and the
springing of one of the arches is encased in later stonework
at the far end of the hall. The building was probably covered
by a steeply pitched roof sloping down to a low wall.

In the 15th century, this low wall on the courtyard front
was replaced with a much higher wall set with large windows.
At the same time, a new roof of much lower pitch was
erected. It rested on the arcade preserved from the earlier
building. In both the old and new halls, heating was provided
by open fires in the centre of the room. Two square hearths
– probably one each from the earlier and later halls – are
visible in the centre of the room.

INTERIOR OF THE HALL

The whole household had access to and ate their meals in
the great hall. The Percy household was so large that food
would probably have been served in several sittings. The hall
had so-called 'low' and 'high' ends. Everyone was seated and
fed in strict order of rank at tables set the length of the
room. The low end was next to the service rooms, the doors
to which were hidden behind a timber screen forming a
corridor known as the screens passage. (A fixing socket for
the screen is visible above head height beside the Lion Tower
entrance door.) The most junior household members sat next
to this screen. At the opposite end of the room was the high
end or dais, where a high table was set across the width of
the room. Access to the dais was a strictly regulated privilege.

A door to the withdrawing chambers, a suite of domestic
rooms for the head of the household, opened off the dais.
Typically, each withdrawing room here was more exclusive

than the last. The first and most important was a grand entertaining room called the great chamber, which in medieval houses was usually set at first-floor level. At Warkworth, a stair connected the dais with the great chamber. In about 1200, this stair rose from the door to the right of the dais and was set within the thickness of the curtain wall. In the 15th century, a grander stair was incorporated within the Little Stair Tower.

4 LITTLE STAIR TOWER

The Little Stair Tower, with its distinctive spire, was a secondary porch to the fourth earl's residence in the bailey. It served the great chamber much as the Lion Tower served the great hall. It was heavily reconsolidated and partly rebuilt in the 1920s. At ground level, the tower incorporated two connected corridors. One of these led into the range from a door opening from the bailey. The other led from the dais of the great hall and had an elegantly vaulted ceiling. A staircase (now lost) rose from it to the first-floor room of the tower. This was the anteroom to the great chamber, where guests would wait for an audience with the earl. It was richly treated, with a fine doorway and a complex vault, the stubs of which remain. The anteroom also had a large window and a recess of uncertain function, both now partially blocked. On the second floor, reached up a spiral stair, was a small domestic chamber with a fireplace.

Below: This photograph shows the Little Stair Tower, on the left, in the late 19th century. The tower was extensively repaired in the 1920s

5 6 GREAT CHAMBER AND CARRICKFERGUS TOWER

The chamber block was a two-storey building at the south-west angle of the bailey. As first constructed in about 1200, the ground-floor room was lit by a series of narrow windows overlooking the bailey. These have since been blocked, but their stepped sills are still visible. Running down the centre of the room are stone bases for the wooden posts that supported the floor of the great chamber above.

The shelf in the curtain wall to the right indicates the position of the great chamber floor. In about 1200, there were probably several large windows in the lost upper storey of the bailey wall on the left. One large window was also set in the curtain wall above the early staircase from the hall. Provided with window seats, it is decorated on the outside with an ornamented stone panel, or tympanum. A ragged hole in the wall beside this window is all that remains of the fireplace of the great chamber.

There was access at both ground- and first-floor levels between the chamber block and the polygonal Carrickfergus Tower in the south-west angle of the curtain wall. The interior of this tower (now visible only from outside the castle) had two upper floors comfortably appointed with latrines and a large fireplace. It may have been to the safety of this tower that the constable of the castle and his son hauled saddlebags loaded with bullion in 1297 (see page 36).

Above: The back of the Little Stair Tower. At ground level to the right is the thick wall of the first great chamber block, built in about 1200
Below: The polygonal Carrickfergus Tower at the south-west corner of the castle – it collapsed in the 18th century

With the addition of the Little Stair Tower in about 1480, the great chamber was recast. The upper part of the bailey wall was demolished and a new facade with large windows built beyond it to enlarge and lighten the interior. The lower part of the old wall was retained, and the space between it and the new facade at ground level became an enclosed passage. Scars in the angle of the curtain wall behind the Carrickfergus Tower show that at the same time a roof of gentle slope replaced the steeply pitched one of about 1200.

Built into the outer wall of the Little Stair Tower are a cupboard and a fireplace. These must have served a small domestic room built above the great chamber in the 1480s. Set on the level of the leads of the roof – an area commonly used in great medieval houses for recreation – this room may have been a banqueting or retiring chamber.

7 SOUTH RANGE

The south range, to the right of the chamber block, formerly stood two storeys high. Occupying one half of the ground floor, and reached down a stair from the great chamber, was a large room with a substantial fireplace (now a ragged hole in the wall). This may once have served as a parlour or retiring chamber, though the remains of grindstones in the ground suggest that it was later used for milling grain. Another large chamber with a fireplace above this room was possibly a balcony overlooking the other half of the building, which was a chapel. Domestic chapels often had such comfortable viewing closets, separating a lord from his household. Part of the door giving direct access from the great chamber to the closet survives. The chapel, which rose through both storeys of the range, can be identified by the piscina, or liturgical basin, in the north wall. It is possible that a reference in a document of 1428 to the foundation of a chantry in the castle is connected to the construction of the chapel and south range.

8 MONTAGU TOWER

The Montagu Tower lies in the south-east corner of the bailey, beyond the gatehouse. Judging by its name and architectural details, this tower was probably erected by John Neville, Lord Montagu, who was earl of Northumberland from 1464 to 1469. Provided with fireplaces and latrines, the upper floors of the tower presumably served as accommodation for senior members of the household. A survey of 1567 describes three 'lodgings' on the upper floors and records that the basement was used as a stable.

Between the Montagu Tower and the gatehouse are the foundations of two successive ranges of medieval buildings of unknown function. The curtain wall behind them was reconstructed in the 1530s and again in the late 18th century.

Below: The exterior of the Montagu Tower. Its upper floors probably housed members of the earl of Northumberland's household in the 15th and 16th centuries, and its basement served as a stable

Above: The sale of horses in a detail of a French manuscript from about 1412 – this is a rare depiction of medieval stables

9 10 STABLE AND WELL HOUSE

Against the east curtain wall, to the left of the Montagu Tower, are the foundations of the great stable. Throughout the Middle Ages, horses would have been bred and trained for many purposes including war, hunting, and drawing carriages or carts. They were stabled and fed according to their value. In 1512, the fifth earl of Northumberland had 33 horses for his own use, and his retinue would have needed many more. When he moved from place to place, it took 17 carriages to transport his household goods.

Survey descriptions record that the upper floor or roof space of the stable served as a granary. Immediately behind the stable in the curtain wall is a small latrine tower, lit inside by small quatrefoil openings. It was probably constructed with the Montagu Tower in the mid-15th century. The square foundation set with drains that stands in front of the stable is all that remains of the main well house. This would have been a timber-framed building with a hoist and a counterweight to draw the water. The drainage holes in the well house platform may have opened into a trough for watering the horses.

11 COLLEGIATE CHURCH

Running across the bailey from east to west, at the foot of the motte, are the foundations of a church. The building is cruciform in plan, and has been curiously squeezed within the bailey, so that most of its elements – such as the transepts and arcades – are absurdly small. Only the east end of the building was designed to any scale, with a high altar and choir and two large crypts beneath. The passage under the choir was the only access between the bailey and the great tower.

The first documentary reference to the church is in 1534, when timber was cleared from the 'college' church and several paintings of saints, almost certainly chapel furnishings, were removed from the castle. At this time the building evidently stood incomplete. To judge from the architectural details of the church and its physical relationship to the Lion Tower, it seems likely to have been begun by the fourth earl as part of his reorganisation of the castle in the 1480s, and was abandoned unfinished after his murder in 1489.

12 GREY MARE'S TAIL TOWER

In the mound beneath the great tower is the ruin of a small, rectangular brewhouse and bakehouse mentioned in the 1567 survey. Brewing and baking often took place in the same building because both processes used yeast and barley.
To the right, in the curtain wall, is the polygonal Grey Mare's Tail Tower; its name is of uncertain origin. Unusually, the arrowloops on each face rise unbroken through two storeys (see page 35) while the arrangement of openings inside relates to the two floors. In the later Middle Ages, one of the arrowloops was infilled with a fireplace, presumably indicating that the tower then served as a lodging. There is a medieval graffito depicting the Crucifixion and a cluster of heads within the grilled opening at ground level on the left-hand side. In 2005, a timber embedded across the head of the same opening was dated using a carbon-dating technique called 'wiggle-matching'. This confirmed that the tower was erected in the 1290s. It may have been built by masons engaged by Edward I in building the royal castle at nearby Berwick.

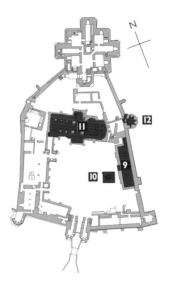

THE CHURCH

1 Choir

2 Crossing

3 Transepts

4 Nave

5 Crypt

6 Passage connecting bailey and great tower

GREAT TOWER

The great tower of Warkworth Castle is a masterpiece of medieval English architecture. It was commissioned by Henry Percy after he was made first earl of Northumberland in 1377. There is a compelling case for attributing its design to the master mason of Durham Priory (now Durham Cathedral), John Lewyn. The building is arranged in the shape of a Greek cross, with four polygonal wings radiating from a central block. As a clerk surveying the castle in 1567 observed, the wings and central block 'be so quarterly squared together that in the sight every part appeareth five towers very finely wrought of masonry work'. Above it rises a viewing tower with magnificent prospects over land and sea.

To understand the full impact of the great tower in the Middle Ages it is necessary to imagine its lost crown of battlements, pinnacles, chimneys and turrets (see page 18). It is possible that the busy outline these created was further enriched with ornamental stone figures of fighting men. Sculptures of angels holding shields survive around the top of the building, and to the north a gigantic Percy lion overlooks the main street of the town. Doubtless all these were painted to make them stand out. The varying size and ornament of the windows indicate the importance of the rooms they light.

How the great tower functioned in conjunction with the hall range in the bailey is not clear. The earls probably used the latter for extended periods of residence with their greater household and the great tower for shorter visits. The only list of its chambers occurs in an undated inventory attached to a survey of 1574. The great tower outlived every other part of the castle, but in 1672 it was stripped of lead and timber and left to ruin. In the 1850s, the architect Anthony Salvin restored the tower and reroofed one corner of it, creating two furnished chambers on the second floor, now known as the Duke's Rooms (see page 46).

Above: The size and ornament of the windows on the second floor of the great tower indicate the high status of the rooms within

Below: The great tower was laid out using a unit of measurement of 16ft 6in., variously called a rod, pole or perch. This is clearly shown in this plan of the first floor of the tower superimposed by a grid of half-rods. The building has distorted slightly over time, but the grey shading shows the planned outline. Building contracts of the period often quantify masonry by the rod so using this unit would have helped in calculating costs and materials

Facing page: A view of the great tower from across the bailey

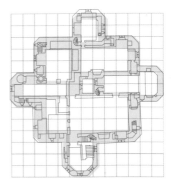

RECONSTRUCTION OF THE GREAT TOWER IN ABOUT 1400

1 Porter's lodge

2 Entrance hall

3 Accounting room with floor safe

4 Lobby

5 Screens passage

6 Great hall

7 Oriel window and stair to wine cellar

8 Buttery

9 Pantry

10 Kitchens

11 Light well

12 Viewing tower

🔢 Ground floor

The modern entrance stair to the great tower stands on the foundation of a medieval predecessor and is overlooked by a worn sculpture of a Percy lion set in a window frame. In its present form the doorway, which was protected by a portcullis, is largely the creation of the restoration work of the 1850s. Within the threshold of the entrance lobby there opened a deep pit, now floored over in timber.

Opening onto the lobby is a tiny porter's lodge in the thickness of the wall, with its own fireplace and drain, probably a urinal. The spacious, vaulted hall beyond is lit at the far end by a window opening into a light well at the centre of the building. Rainwater from the roof drained into the light well and could be either collected in a cistern or flushed through the latrine chutes.

Around the entrance hall is a warren of vaulted service and storage chambers. To the left of the hall is an accounting room with a large floor safe (now floored over in timber) for valuables. Opening off this is a wall chamber with a fireplace, window, latrine and wall basin, probably for the use of a senior financial officer of the household. The other basement rooms functioned as storage spaces for the chambers on the floors above, to which they are connected by narrow stairs: the beer cellar to the buttery, the wine cellars to the high table in the great hall, and a room for fuel and food to the main kitchen. One room is described in the inventory made about 1574 as a bedroom for the boy servants.

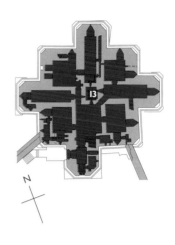

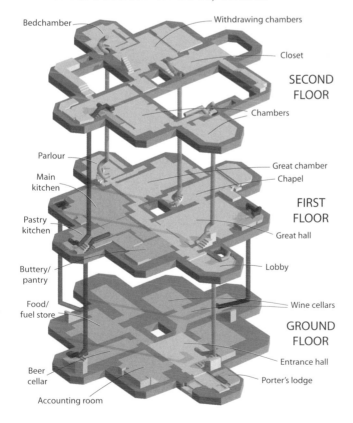

Left: The great tower is a brilliant piece of three-dimensional design, incorporating different sizes and heights of chamber within a regular external volume. It also connects service chambers (pink) with domestic ones (yellow) by an ingenious system of wall stairs. Access between floors is indicated by the pink and yellow lines

⁴ Staircase and lobby

The main stair to the first floor is housed in the wing of the building projecting to the south. At the foot of the stair is a small chamber with a drain. This was probably a washing room for visitors but it might also have been a urinal. The stair rises to a spacious lobby, with stone benches and a fireplace. Lit by large, glazed windows, it was effectively an internal porch, where visitors to the earl's state apartments on this floor could wait in warmth and comfort. A square opening in the wall to the right of the fireplace allowed the portcullis for the main entrance below to be raised and pegged open.

Access to the rooms beyond the stair and porch would have been carefully regulated – an official would have sat on a stone bench in a niche to the left of the door from the landing. From here he could oversee both the entrance to the great hall and the door opposite his seat, which opens on to a stair rising to a set of chambers on the floor above – two of these rooms are now known as the Duke's Rooms. The inventory taken about 1574 describes these as including a 'clerk's chamber', which suggests that they served as offices for the earl's household administration.

There was a tradition of large entrance stairs to great towers in England that extended back to the 12th century. This particular arrangement, however, was probably informed by Edward III's rebuilding of Windsor Castle from the 1350s.

Above: *The main stair in the great tower, leading up to the lobby and great hall*
Right: *View into the lobby from the great hall – the three doorways on the right lead to the kitchens, buttery and pantry*

15 Great hall

This interior was arranged exactly as was the great hall in the bailey. From the lobby, the visitor passed into a screens passage. On the left are the three doors to the kitchens, buttery and pantry. The hall was covered by a massive timber roof of low pitch, as shown by the surviving gables. Above the dais at the 'high' end of the room are two high windows connected by a passage in the thickness of the wall. This may have formed a viewing loft or musicians' gallery.

A single window on the left, opening on to the light well, illuminates the interior. In the opposite wall there were originally two tall windows. That at the far end was the largest, lighting the high table. It incorporates a door leading up from the wine cellar in the basement, and a stone niche. This niche probably served as a sideboard for the linen, cutlery and cups used at the high table. The second window, later infilled with a fireplace, is visible only in outline.

This new fireplace made the hearth in the centre of the room redundant. It also rendered unnecessary the original and bizarre system of smoke extraction: at the head of each window is a small rectangular opening that served as a flue. Another example of this unusual arrangement is found at Bolton Castle in Yorkshire, another building associated with John Lewyn. Observing this at Bolton, the 16th-century writer John Leland marvelled: 'by this means is the smoke of the hearth wonder strangely conveyed from the hall'.

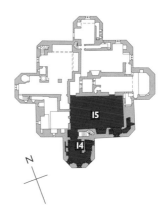

THE GREAT HALL

1 Position of dais

2 Door to wine cellar

3 Window opening, later blocked with fireplace

4 Corbel at apex of hall roof

5 Door to chapel

6 Windows with wall passage

Above: A queen watches from the privacy of a closet – in this case a fabric tent – as the priest performs the Mass

THE CHAPEL

1 Sedile, or seat for the priest celebrating the Mass

2 Piscina, or liturgical basin

3 Sacristy with squints (viewing slits) overlooking the altar

4 Corbel supporting the floor of the balcony closet

16 Chapel

At the high end of the hall a doorway on the left leads to the chapel. This consists of a narrow nave and a raised altar space encircled by windows. The corbels in the walls of the nave show that the interior was originally divided into two floors, the upper one forming a deep balcony overlooking the altar. This balcony, reached from the withdrawing chambers on the floor above, had a fireplace and would have served as a closet where the earl could perform his devotions in private.

Other members of the household wishing to observe the celebration of the Mass presumably occupied the nave, which was lit only from a window opening on to the central light well. But the nave must also have doubled as a thoroughfare: immediately opposite the door from the hall is the outline of a blocked door that once led to the great chamber beyond. A second door, beside the light well at the inner end of the nave to the left, gave access to the closet and withdrawing apartments above. Beside it is either a basin or a urinal.

The altar was set on a dais in the east end of the chapel, now laid with some reset medieval tiles probably dating to about 1500. The windows would have been filled with stained glass. Between the windows are angel corbels for large statues, and to the right of the altar are the liturgical seat and basin used by the priest in the Mass. Next to these is a door into a small sacristy, complete with a stone table for laying out vestments. Various squints, or narrow openings, in the sacristy overlook the altar, which suggest that this room also served as a private closet. To the left of the altar is a small door that leads via a lobby to the great chamber.

17 Great chamber

The original main entrance to the great chamber was probably the blocked door to the chapel nave visible in the wall to the left. Privileged visitors used this doorway to reach the great chamber from the high table in the hall. The great chamber was a formal reception room, the first and grandest in the sequence of the earl's four withdrawing chambers in the great tower. Its walls would have been covered with expensive fabric hangings or tapestries, and its ceiling was probably richly carved and painted.

The earl's suite was arranged on two floors, with an identical pair of chambers on each. All four chambers had low ceilings and dedicated latrines. The fireplaces and wall sockets for the timbers indicate the floor level of the upper chambers. There are two doors at the far end of the great chamber. That to the right opens onto a tiny nest of doors: one gives on to a stair to the rooms above and the roof; another to a latrine down a long passage; and a third into a room within the northern wing, possibly a parlour. The room on the floor above the great chamber served as a private retiring room for the earl and his close companions. Above the parlour was the most exclusive room in the tower, probably the earl's bedchamber. In a building with windows advertising the disposition of rooms, it can be no coincidence that this room is marked outside with the great Percy lion.

Above: A 15th-century French manuscript illumination depicting Charles VI, king of France, conversing with his secretary and courtiers. The earl of Northumberland's great chamber at Warkworth would also have been sumptuously furnished

Feeding the Household

The castle kitchens had to produce food for the entire household according to rank

The remarkably well-preserved kitchens at Warkworth testify to the sophisticated cooking arrangements within a great medieval household. Deep fireplaces allowed for the use of spits, grills and cauldrons. Flexibility was important in kitchens that prepared both a huge quantity and a great variety of food every day. The members of the household received regular doles of bread and beer. Both were stored near the hall: bread in the pantry and beer in the buttery. These rooms, supervised respectively by the pantler and butler, take their names respectively from 'pain', the French word for bread, and 'butt', or barrel.

The early 16th-century Northumberland Household Book describes the food allocated to each member of the household. It provides details of four different types of meal and, in each case, the ten different portions to be prepared. Of these, the most magnificent went to the earl and countess. During Lent, for example, they received for breakfast measures of beer and wine with portions of salted fish, herring and sprats, as well as bread. For the same meal, the gentlemen of the household were each given a loaf of bread, a measure of beer and a piece of salted fish.

Just as in a restaurant, the preparation and service of food were undertaken by several teams of staff, each with their own responsibilities. Where possible these teams worked in demarcated areas and passed dishes across counters. By creating handover points it was possible to check every stage in the preparation of a dish on its way to the table, and to ensure that food – a massive household expense – did not go missing.

Above: A 16th-century illustration showing the preparation of food for the winter

Below: A cook and scullion roasting poultry in a kitchen, in a detail from a 14th-century manuscript

ⓘ Kitchens, buttery and pantry

Today, the kitchens comprise two rooms. These were formerly divided into three working areas, each with its own dedicated staff. At the entrance to the kitchens was a servery. The cooks in the main kitchen probably passed dishes over a low counter set in the larger of the two arches, where waiters collected them to carry to the hall. The smaller arch was a door to the main kitchen. At the far end of the servery, partitioned by a screen (now lost), was a pastry kitchen. It was provided with an oven and cauldron stand, both set inside an opening similar to a fireplace. A tiny room over the oven perhaps served as a drying space. Above the servery and pastry kitchen was one of the series of chambers probably used by senior household officials. They could have monitored activity in the kitchen using a stair leading down to the window of the pastry kitchen. The level of the lost upper floor is indicated by wall sockets.

To relieve the intense heat from its two huge fireplaces, the main kitchen rose through two storeys. Above one of the fireplaces is a wall chamber, perhaps a drying room or a bedchamber. A stair beside the window descends to the basement, where huge quantities of food and firewood were stored. A small room on the opposite side of the window was probably a store for the more valuable ingredients.

Cut through the outer wall is a deep drain for water for washing out the kitchen, probably covered formerly by a grille. A small opening in the wall above gave cooks in the main kitchen access to a boiling cauldron heated on a fire in the pastry kitchen. The pantry and buttery between the kitchens and the hall today form a single chamber with two doors, but originally a timber partition divided them. A wall stair leads down from the buttery to the beer cellar.

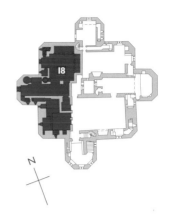

THE KITCHENS

1 Servery area

2 Position of kitchen counter

3 Position of screen

4 Pastry kitchen

5 Oven

6 Cauldron stand

7 Drains

8 Socket for upper chamber floor

Below: A view from the south-east of the gatehouse and castle ditch, both restored in the 1920s

19 GATEHOUSE

The gatehouse, reached by retracing your route out of the great tower and across the bailey, was built in about 1200 as a formidable defence for the main entrance to the bailey. Its internal facade, however, was domestic in character. The upper chamber had large windows overlooking the bailey and was described in 1538 as the bedchamber of the earl himself. At ground level are the remains of five archways. The central and largest one opens onto the main gateway. To either side are doorways into the ground-floor chambers which, according to the 1567 survey, served as a porter's lodge and a prison. Each of the outer arches is a doorway to stairs. The gate-passage is covered by a pointed barrel vault cut through with murder holes, for dropping missiles on attackers. At the outer end it was closed by a portcullis, secured against a step, and an outward-opening gate. Both details are unusual and are paralleled in the postern gate of the same date.

The front of the gatehouse comprises a pair of polygonal towers with buttresses of the same form at each front corner. Beautifully integrated within this design is a series of small arrowloops, their bases splayed to afford the maximum field of fire. Above the gate-passage are stone brackets for a fighting platform, probably added in about 1400. At the same level in the towers to either side is a series of sockets, probably the fixings for additional timber fortifications.

After the castle fell into ruin, the gatehouse was adapted as a custodian's house. These additions were stripped away when the property was taken into state care, and the gatehouse was restored to its present form in the 1920s.

WARKWORTH TOWN

A path to the right of the exit from the gatehouse leads
down a flight of steps and along the west curtain wall of the
castle to the town. The castle shelters the town beneath,
closing its circuit of river defence and forming with it a
formidable military and civilian stronghold. Few places in
England preserve so strong a sense of their medieval layout.

The entrance to the town was over the river at the tip of
the Warkworth peninsula. The late 14th-century fortified
bridge is a rare survival. In the centre of the bridge there
once stood a stone cross (see page 45), which was torn
down and thrown into the river in the 19th century. From
the bridge, the main street runs past the parish church of
St Lawrence, where it widens to create a market place. The
church became a cell of Durham Priory in the 12th century
and has a remarkable vaulted chancel dating from this period.

From the market place, the main road rises up the hill
towards the castle and goes past it into the countryside.
Behind the houses that line the street extend long, narrow
gardens, vestiges of the medieval property divisions of the
town. The park, its game jealously guarded for the sport of
hunting, formerly extended to the west of Warkworth. Set
within this and easily accessible from the castle was the
hermitage, a religious foundation of the Percy family. Today
it is reached by boat via the path from the castle.

*Above: A map of Warkworth
showing the layout of the town and
hermitage. The park lay to the west
of the castle on the far side of the
river. It is first documented in 1749
as a small enclosure of woodland
'half a league in circuit' but was
greatly enlarged in the 1480s*
Below: *The market place and main
street of Warkworth in about 1900,
looking towards the castle*

Above: The ruins of Warkworth Hermitage depicted in a watercolour of 1798 by Thomas Girtin. It shows the ruins of the priest's house (right) and the small closet at the west end of the chapel (left)

THE HERMITAGE

A surveyor describing the estate around Warkworth Castle in 1567 noted, 'There is in the Park also one house hewn within a crag which is called the Hermitage Chapel. In the same has been one priest kept, which did such godly service as at that time was used and celebrated.' This extraordinary rock-cut chapel survives, together with the remains of a small domestic building for the priest. It is a remarkable and atmospheric site, shrouded by trees from the outside world.

THE FOUNDATION AND ITS PRIESTS

The hermitage was almost certainly established as a votive chapel in about 1400 by the first earl of Northumberland in conjunction with his work to the castle. There is no documentary proof of this, but two factors stand in favour of it. First, there are several comparable rock-cut chapels from this period in England, notably Guy's Chapel at Warwick, rebuilt in 1423, and the Chapel of Our Lady at Knaresborough, Yorkshire, founded in 1408. Secondly, the hermitage was dedicated to the Trinity, and its internal ornament reflects particular devotion to the Virgin Mary. The first earl solemnly invoked the Trinity and the Virgin in 1373 when confirming a bequest to Alnwick Abbey.

The first documentary reference to the hermitage occurs in 1487, when a certain Thomas Barker was described as 'chaplain of the chantry in Sunderland Park'. Confusingly, this implies that, despite its name, the hermitage probably never functioned as a secluded dwelling for a religious recluse. Rather, it was a privately established chapel or chantry, where an ordinary priest performed services in return for a stipend from the earl.

Nothing is known of the terms of service to the chapel, which may have changed over time, but the names of several priests associated with the hermitage are recorded. Thomas Barker was appointed to his post for life by the fourth earl of Northumberland, and in 1487 he received licence to graze cattle in the surrounding park. John Greene and Edward Slegges are described as serving the Chapel of the Holy Trinity in the park in 1506 and 1515 respectively. The last-known priest of the hermitage was George Lancastre, chaplain to the sixth earl. He was appointed on 3 December 1531, with a good salary of 20 marks and other benefits. These included use of pasture for his livestock, a garden and an orchard near the hermitage, a draught of fish every Sunday and 20 loads of firewood.

THE HERMITAGE AFTER THE REFORMATION

After the Reformation of the mid-16th century, the hermitage was abandoned and over time its remains became objects of curiosity and romance. The publication in 1771 by Bishop Percy of a ballad entitled *The Hermit of Warkworth* brought about its popular rediscovery. Percy was a scholarly antiquarian but his narrative – which tells the tale of a knight disappointed in love who retired from the world – was based on the Nativity scene in the chapel being incorrectly identified as a woman's tomb. His poem was a success and was ferociously parodied by Samuel Johnson.

Above: The ferryman rowing his boat across the river to the hermitage
Left: The frontispiece to Bishop Percy's The Hermit of Warkworth *(1771). The publication of this ballad led to renewed interest in the hermitage*

EXTERIOR

A path from the landing stage leads to the hermitage, and a modern stair against the cliff face provides access to the rock-cut chambers. The stair stands within the foundations of a low, ruined building, possibly a kitchen: to the right of the platform at the turn of the steps are the remains of an oven. Cut into the cliff face above is a small door and a raised stair that leads to the top of the cliff, probably giving access to the garden and orchard that formed part of the property. To the left of the cliff are the remains of a ruined two-storey building, presumably the priest's house.

A small porch encloses the door to the hermitage chapel. At each side is a small niche, formerly fitted with a wooden seat. Immediately above the door is a roughly executed carving of the Crucifixion, with Christ flanked by the Virgin and St John. Antiquarian accounts record that there was a short painted inscription from Psalm 42 over the door: 'My tears have been my meat day and night.'

CHAPEL

The chapel was carved directly out of the rock. It comprises three vaulted bays, each defined by a roughly carved shaft rising up the wall. A series of plain bosses ornaments the intersection of the vaulting ribs in every bay. On a worn step at the far end is the altar, and above it is a niche for a small statue. Early engravings record over this niche the outline in paint of a figure with a cruciform halo emblematic of Christ.

By the window, to the right of the altar, is a cluster of rough

Above: An alabaster depicting the Trinity in a 15th-century altarpiece. From the dedication of the chapel and the recorded detail of a cruciform halo on the wall, it is likely that an image in this form was set in the niche above the altar of the hermitage
Right: The modern entrance stair to the hermitage chapel cut in the cliff face. To the right of the landing are the remains of an oven

and worn sculptures forming an almost life-size Nativity scene.
The Virgin Mary, lying down, is at the centre, carrying in her
arms the infant Christ, now little more than a lump of stone.
From behind her head and feet emerge the heads of the ox
and ass. At her feet stands Joseph, leaning on a staff. There is
a pedestal in the wall beneath the sculpture, and a basin,
possibly a stoup for holy water; in the next bay.

INNER CHAMBER

Facing the entrance to the chapel is a doorway to an inner
chamber. Over this is a shield carved with the instruments of
Christ's Passion – the scourge, cross, nails and sponge. An
18th-century description notes that fragments of an inscription
from Psalm 69 were visible around this shield: 'They gave me gall
for my meat and in my thirst they gave me vinegar to drink.'

The inner chamber, with a barrel-vaulted ceiling, is much
plainer than the chapel, though it follows the same basic
design, with a raised altar – now badly damaged – at its east
end. To the right of the altar is a small niche, probably a
piscina, or liturgical basin. Conventionally identified as a
sacristy, the chamber is more likely to have been a closet
for the earl and his retinue, as there are viewing slits and
windows cut in the wall adjoining the chapel.

Leading from the closet is a small chamber at the back of
the chapel, again with openings in the wall allowing people to
watch the Mass. In the late 18th century a pillar 'of very
picturesque appearance' was described as once standing
between the chapel and closet. Whether such a pillar existed,
or where it stood, is not clear today.

*Above left: The doorway to the inner
chamber of the chapel, probably a
viewing closet for the earl and his
retinue. On the shield above the
door are carved the instruments
of the Passion*

*Above right: The chapel of the
hermitage, carved out of the rock*

*Below: The disposition of figures in
the curved Nativity scene in the
hermitage chapel at Warkworth is
precisely the same as that in this
French manuscript illumination of
the 14th century*

History

Probably founded in about 1200, Warkworth became one of the most important castles in northern England. It was the favoured residence of the powerful Percy family from the 14th to the 17th centuries.

READING THE HISTORY

This section describes the history of Warkworth Castle and the Percy family up to the present day. It includes a feature on the caretakers of the castle in the early 20th century (page 47).

ANGLO-SAXON AND NORMAN WARKWORTH

The castle and town of Warkworth occupy a naturally
fortified site less than a mile from the Northumberland coast.
There is evidence for prehistoric settlement in the area,
notably a Neolithic rock-cut 'cup-and-ring' sculpture in the
river cliffs to the north of the town, but Warkworth itself is
first mentioned in the Anglo-Saxon period. In 737, Ceolwulf,
king of Northumbria, resigned his crown and joined the
monastic community of Lindisfarne, on Holy Island. To
mark the event, he bestowed numerous properties on
the monastery, including Warkworth, then described as
Werceworde, meaning 'the homestead of Werce'. The grant
specifically included the present parish church of St Lawrence,
which Ceolwulf had founded.

*Above: The church of St Lawrence at
Warkworth, founded by Ceolwulf,
king of Northumbria*

More than a century later, Warkworth was seized back
from the monastery by the last king of Northumbria, Osbert,
who was killed fighting the Danes in 867. Subsequent control of
it appears to have passed by descent through the powerful earls
of Northumbria. Little is known about the late Anglo-Saxon
settlement at Warkworth, but there was probably a residence
belonging to the earls on the site. After the Norman Conquest
of 1066, there are several references to bequests of property
from the manor to local religious foundations, including those at
Tynemouth, Brinkburn and Alnwick.

*Below: An aerial view of Warkworth
from the south-west, showing the
long medieval burgage plots, or
property divisions, of the town*

*Facing page: Detail of a view
of Warkworth Castle (exhibited in
1799) by J M W Turner*

Above: The castle of Bamburgh, an ancient seat of royal authority in northern England. Earl Henry of Northumberland owned it in the mid-12th century

Below: A silver penny minted in Carlisle for Earl Henry, between 1139 and 1153. During the civil war between the Empress Matilda and King Stephen, rival claimants to the English throne, the nobility were granted the right to issue coins in return for their support

THE FOUNDATION OF THE CASTLE

The first mention of Warkworth Castle occurs in the middle of the 12th century. Between 1157 and 1164, a charter of Henry II granted to one Roger fitz Eustace the castle and manor of Warkworth. It has been argued that the castle Roger received had been established 20 years earlier by Henry, the son of David I, king of Scotland. Henry became earl of Northumberland under the Treaty of Durham in 1139, and he has conventionally been credited with raising the motte and bailey and the first stone buildings at Warkworth to serve as the seat of his authority in the region. This was necessary because the treaty also stipulated that the English king should retain Bamburgh and Newcastle, the principal castles of the region.

But the case for supposing that Earl Henry was the founder of Warkworth Castle is not clear-cut. Charters issued by Earl Henry from Bamburgh illustrate that, despite the terms of the Treaty of Durham, that castle did in fact come into his possession. In which case, it would not have been necessary for him to build at Warkworth. There is also a circumstantial problem with this attribution. Judging by Henry II's grant, the castle that Roger received came with a small estate, much diminished since the reign of Ceolwulf. Events in the 1170s also show that its fortifications were limited. It is unlikely that Earl Henry would have founded a castle so modest and with such a small estate.

Two different explanations present themselves. It is possible that the castle was actually built in the 1150s to consolidate Henry II's repossession of Northumberland in 1157, an action that certainly led to the building of similar motte-and-bailey castles nearby, such as Harbottle. Alternatively, the charter may have simply dignified the ancient residence at the centre of the manor of Warkworth with the title of a castle.

ROGER FITZ EUSTACE

Roger, to whom Henry II granted the castle, was a rich man with far-flung estates and probably little concerned with Warkworth. But he was in Northumberland during the invasion of 1173 led by William the Lion, king of Scotland. According to the Scottish chronicler Jordan Fantosme, Roger made no attempt to defend Warkworth because its walls, ditches and earthworks were 'feeble'. He remained instead at Newcastle to repel the invasion. The following year, Warkworth was attacked by the earl of Fife, who allegedly massacred the population, including those who took sanctuary in the church. Perhaps because of its weak defences, the castle is not even mentioned in the record of that event.

ROBERT FITZ ROGER AND HIS DESCENDANTS

Roger died in 1178, while his son, Robert, was still a child. When Robert came of age in 1191, his interests were chiefly vested in Norfolk, where he had a substantial inheritance. But from 1199 onwards he became increasingly active in Northumberland. In that year, for the sum of 300 marks, he purchased royal confirmation of his ownership of both the castle and the manor of Warkworth. A favourite of King John, he became in 1203 sheriff of Northumberland, and a powerful royal official. Later, the king granted him land in the county. In 1213, the year before his death, he received the king at Warkworth.

The present castle at Warkworth, including its motte and bailey, may essentially be the creation of Robert, between 1199 and 1214. Preserved in the fortifications are many features that might be associated with him, including the gatehouse, Carrickfergus Tower, postern gate and east curtain wall. The spur walls are also likely to date from this time and suggest that the present great tower replaced an earlier stone structure. One recurrent feature of the 13th-century work is the use of polygonal buttresses, a form first found in northern English architecture in the late 12th century.

Robert's son, John, succeeded his father in 1214 and possibly completed the work to the castle. When he died in 1240, his son, Roger, was still a child. Roger was trampled to death during a tournament in 1249, leaving a son, Robert, aged only one and a half. Robert and his estates were committed to the custody of William de Valence, half-brother of Henry III. Recording this, the chronicler Matthew Paris described Warkworth as a 'noble castle'. Clearly the buildings were much altered from their state in 1173.

Below: *The Grey Mare's Tail Tower (left), built in the 1290s. Its details relate to Edward I's works at Berwick. The spur wall rising up the motte to the great tower was probably built by Robert fitz Roger between 1199 and 1214*

Above: A 14th-century manuscript illustration of John de Balliol as king of Scotland, acknowledging the overlordship of Edward I, king of England. Edward's intervention in Scottish affairs plunged the two kingdoms into centuries of conflict

Below: This seal bears the arms of Percy 'ancient'. The matrix of this seal was ceremonially smashed at Warkworth on 18 July 1343. By this act the second Lord Percy formally assumed a rampant lion as his new heraldic device. It was a fashionable emblem in Edward III's court, and so also proclaimed Percy's political ambition in the North

THE ANGLO-SCOTTISH WARS

The events of Edward I's reign (1272–1307) were to transform life along the Anglo-Scottish border. Edward – who stayed at Warkworth for one night in 1292 – was invited to arbitrate in a dispute over the Scottish throne, and used the opportunity to claim overlordship of the kingdom. The result was a long-running war between England and Scotland.

Robert, owner of Warkworth, became closely involved in the Anglo-Scottish wars and was captured, together with his son, John, after the English defeat at Stirling in 1297. During their absence from the castle on campaign, the constable of Warkworth took receipt of money on behalf of a servant of Hugh de Cressingham, the treasurer of England. Cressingham was killed at Stirling, and the delivery of the money became a matter of dispute. In 1304 the constable testified that he had received exceedingly heavy saddlebags of money from one of the treasurer's servants and that he and his son had carried them from the great chamber to an adjacent closet, probably in the Carrickfergus Tower. It was also around this time, in the late 1290s, that the Grey Mare's Tail Tower was added to the castle, judging by recent dating of its timber.

Robert's son, John de Clavering, took control of his father's estates in 1310, and in 1311 made over the inheritance of all his property to the king, probably because of his debts: in 1317 he admitted owing the huge sum of £600 to an Italian merchant from Lucca. John's parlous financial position was doubtless exacerbated by the English defeat at Bannockburn in 1314, which opened the border to Scottish attack.

Castles such as Warkworth now began to play an increasingly important role in the war, as their garrisons deterred raids and swelled the numbers of expeditionary forces. As a result, royal funds were directed towards the construction and maintenance of private fortresses. At Warkworth in 1319, for example, the king provided four men-at-arms and eight hobelars, or light cavalry, to serve with the existing garrison of 12 men-at-arms. There are regular references to Warkworth in subsequent years. In 1322, the constable, with 26 hobelars from the garrison, joined the royal army on its march into Scotland. The following year, the king ordered John de Clavering to prepare the defences of the castle, and in 1327 it was besieged by the Scots. The attack was unsuccessful, but in 1341 the Scots sacked the town.

THE PERCYS

John de Clavering died in 1332, but the castle did not pass to the king. In 1328 Edward III had granted it to Henry Percy, second Lord Percy. The Percy family was emerging as one of the most important in the North of England. The castle and barony of Alnwick, which the Percys had bought in 1309, remained their chief holding in Northumberland throughout the Middle Ages. Under the Percys, Warkworth Castle became an architectural showpiece. Whereas Alnwick boasted larger estates and greater prestige, Warkworth was the favoured residence. As a result, in the late Middle Ages it developed two residential complexes of unparalleled quality and sophistication in Northumberland. It also had a small park, where the Percys enjoyed hunting. Neither the second nor third Lord Percy appears to have undertaken much work to the castle, but Henry Percy, first earl of Northumberland (1341–1408), transformed it. He was the first great landowner in the North to acquire a noble title, and he almost certainly celebrated this by building the great tower.

Below: A view of Alnwick Castle in about 1700; the castle is the main residence of the Percy family today. The inner gatehouse of about 1340 in the centre of this painting is ornamented with heraldry and sculptures of fighting men, details possibly copied on the great tower of Warkworth Castle

THE BUILDING OF THE GREAT TOWER

Henry Percy's earldom was in part an acknowledgement of his exceptional status and power across the whole border with Scotland, known as the March. It also reflected his high standing at court, where he had forged a political alliance with John of Gaunt, a son of Edward III and the leading magnate of the realm. The two men were closely allied until 1381, when the crisis of the Peasants' Revolt brought about a violent public quarrel between them. Gaunt was active in the region both before and after this as Lieutenant of the March. He adopted as his seat in the March the nearby castle of Dunstanburgh as his headquarters, altering it for use between 1380 and 1383. Percy too was spurred to build.

In many respects the great tower is characteristic of the North East architectural tradition and bears comparison with a number of late 14th-century buildings in northern England. Notable among these are the castles at Bolton, Sheriff Hutton and Gilling East in Yorkshire, as well as the domestic ranges at nearby Bamburgh Castle. Technical and planning similarities make it virtually certain that the mason John Lewyn was responsible for the work. But the building also shows clear knowledge of the two most important architectural commissions of Edward III's reign: the vast royal palace at Windsor Castle, Berkshire, begun in the late 1350s, and John of Gaunt's great residential ranges at his castle of Kenilworth, Warwickshire, which were largely complete by 1377. The similarities to the latter almost certainly result from the first earl's close connections before 1381 with Gaunt, from whom he may have received architectural drawings or borrowed craftsmen. It is also likely that the first earl established the hermitage at Warkworth in conjunction with his enlargement of the castle.

Above: John of Gaunt, first an ally but later an enemy of the first earl of Northumberland
Right: A view of John of Gaunt's 14th-century additions to Kenilworth Castle, Warwickshire. The distinctive window forms may have influenced the design of the great tower at Warkworth

Left: Richard II (centre) receiving the first earl of Northumberland (left) at Conwy, Wales, in a detail from a late 14th-century manuscript. Despite professing his loyalty, the earl was actively involved in deposing Richard in 1399

THE REBELLION OF THE PERCYS

The first earl of Northumberland played an active role in deposing Richard II in 1399, but he and his son, the famous Harry Hotspur (1364–1403), soon quarrelled with Henry IV, the king they had put on the throne in Richard's place. In 1403, Hotspur was killed at the Battle of Shrewsbury while in open rebellion. The earl, who was marching to meet him, heard of this disaster and fled north to Warkworth, where he had first plotted his treason. Shortly afterwards, he was arrested and his property seized by the king. Enforcing this seizure, however, proved difficult. At Warkworth, the king's officer was met by Percy's 14-year-old son, who declared himself a loyal subject but regretted that he did not have the ceremonial trappings necessary to surrender the castle formally to the king, and on this absurd pretext kept control of it. Embroiled in other domestic troubles and unable to enforce his repeated commands, Henry IV restored the earl to his estates in 1404.

In response, Percy took the first opportunity to show his continued discontent, joining an unsuccessful conspiracy against the king led by Archbishop Scrope in 1405. Having crushed Scrope's rebellion, Henry IV acted decisively, amassing an army and marching north. Percy fled to Scotland as the forces approached, but his castles did put up some resistance. Writing in the comfort of the chambers of the recently captured Warkworth, Henry IV reported to his privy council that the captain had at first refused to surrender the castle, as it was well provisioned and its defences strong. But, after the king's cannon had fired seven shots, the garrison cried for mercy and sued for peace.

Above: Dunstanburgh Castle, adopted by John of Gaunt as his seat of authority in the March. During the Wars of the Roses the castle was held by the House of Lancaster and in 1462 was besieged by the Yorkists, who controlled Warkworth Castle

THE WARS OF THE ROSES

With the Percy family disgraced, its possessions passed to the Crown. Warkworth was occupied intermittently by one of Henry IV's younger sons, John of Lancaster, who served as Warden of the Eastern March. But following the accession of Henry V in 1413, the son of Harry Hotspur, another Henry Percy (1393–1455), was restored to the family inheritance in 1416 as second earl of Northumberland. He resided at Warkworth, and several letters written by him from the castle survive. He undertook building work at the castle, though it is not now clear what this was.

The second earl was killed fighting for the Lancastrian cause of Henry VI at the Battle of St Albans in 1455, at the beginning of the Wars of the Roses. His son, Henry, the third earl (1421–61), suffered a similar fate at the Battle of Towton. Following this defeat, the castles of Northumberland – except Warkworth – played a prominent role as centres of Lancastrian resistance. In 1462, the Yorkist forces, led by the earl of Warwick, simultaneously besieged Bamburgh, Dunstanburgh and Alnwick castles. Warkworth Castle was occupied as the Yorkist headquarters, and Warwick rode out from it every day to supervise the different sieges.

Following the death of the third Percy earl of Northumberland, Edward IV settled the title on the brother of the earl of Warwick, John Neville, Lord Montagu. In 1470, however, he restored the eldest son of the third earl to his inheritance and – in 1471 – to his title. The household accounts of the fourth earl, Henry (c. 1449–1489), indicate that he maintained Warkworth. The heraldic decoration on the Lion Tower also shows that at some time after his

marriage in 1472 he began the complete remodelling of the bailey. The refusal of the fourth earl to commit his following at the Battle of Bosworth in 1485 allowed the Tudor king Henry VII to ascend the throne. For this act the earl was held in popular contempt and he was murdered in 1489, allegedly after his disillusioned household abandoned him to a mob.

THE FIFTH AND SIXTH EARLS

The title and estates then passed to the fourth earl's son, Henry Algernon (c. 1478–1527). The fifth earl maintained the buildings at Warkworth, but evidently abandoned his father's plans for a new collegiate church in the castle. The sixth earl, another Henry Percy (c. 1502–1537), undertook several documented repairs, including the reconstruction of the wall between the gatehouse and the Montagu Tower in 1534, and the clearance of the incomplete church. He lived far beyond his means, however: one Crown official reported that he had never seen a finer inheritance 'more blemished by the folly of its owner or the untruth of his servants'.

The sixth earl died in 1537 without heirs; his brother Sir Thomas Percy had been executed in 1536 for his part in the Pilgrimage of Grace – the rising in northern England against the Suppression of the Monasteries by Henry VIII. Reluctantly, therefore, the sixth earl conveyed his estates to the Crown. His brother's descendants were eventually restored to the Percy inheritance by Mary I in 1557. In the meantime, control of the March passed to a series of appointed royal officers. All made use of Warkworth but none would pay for repairs, and by 1550 the castle was described as rapidly falling into decay for want of basic maintenance.

Above: A view of Warkworth Castle from the west. The outer bailey was completely remodelled by the fourth earl at the end of the 15th century. The fields in the foreground were formerly part of the park
Below: The seal of Henry Algernon Percy, fifth earl of Northumberland

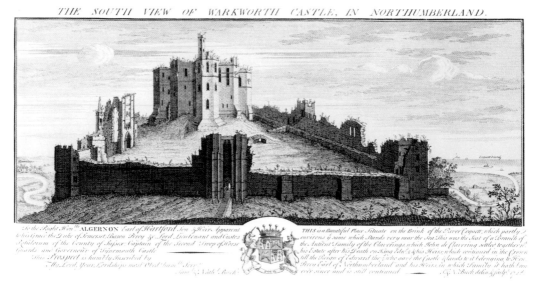

THE SOUTH VIEW OF WARKWORTH CASTLE, IN NORTHUMBERLAND.

Above: An engraving of Warkworth Castle by Samuel and Nathaniel Buck (1728). The castle began to fall into disrepair during the late 16th century, but this view shows the Carrickfergus Tower (bottom left) still complete

THE SEVENTH AND EIGHTH EARLS

That decay was arrested when the sixth earl's nephew, Thomas Percy (c. 1528–1572), was given control of the family estates and restored to the title in 1557. He apparently used the castle quite regularly, and a survey taken in 1567 shows it to have been in reasonable repair. This survey provides the most detailed account of the medieval buildings, and may have been carried out to help plan a substantial reordering of the castle: in 1570, it was reported that 'the hall and other houses of office' in the bailey had been 'taken down' by the earl in preparation for their reconstruction.

Unfortunately, before the work could be completed, the seventh earl was involved in the unsuccessful rising of 1569 that sought to re-establish Roman Catholicism in England under Elizabeth I. During this rising, the two Percy castles, at Warkworth and Alnwick, were filled with servants and tenants sympathetic to the cause. So alarming was this gathering that Sir John Forster, a Warden of the March, issued proclamations at the gates of both castles ordering those within to leave, or face charges of treason. In the campaign that followed the rising, Warkworth Castle was commandeered by the queen's forces. Between their visits, however, Forster took advantage of his office to pillage the castle. In April 1572, Lord Hunsdon wrote to complain of this behaviour to the queen's chief minister, William Cecil, Lord Burghley: 'It is great pity to see how Alnwick Castle and Warkworth are spoiled by him … I am creditably informed that he means utterly to deface both.'

The earl, meanwhile, was a prisoner in Scotland and in July 1572 was sold to Elizabeth I. On 22 August, he was executed in York, and the claims of his son to the Percy inheritance were passed over. But in 1574 the queen relented and allowed Henry (c. 1532–1585), brother of the seventh earl, to assume the title and control of his estates. The survey of the castle that followed shows that parts of the building were now ruinous. Another report also described the damage done to the buildings by the looting of metal as 'great and marvellous'. What repair was undertaken is not clear, but when the ninth earl, Henry (1564–1632), came into possession of Warkworth in 1585, some rooms were clearly habitable. In 1587, his receiver-general was lodging in the castle. The castle was also sufficiently celebrated at the time to be used by Shakespeare as the setting for several scenes of his *Henry IV* plays, written in 1597.

Above: A portrait miniature of the ninth earl of Northumberland by Nicholas Hilliard, from about 1595
Below: Detail from the first page of the First Folio (1623) of Shakespeare's Henry IV, Part 2, several scenes of which were set at Warkworth

SIR RALPH GRAY

Following the discovery of the Gunpowder Plot to blow up the Houses of Parliament in 1605, the ninth earl was arrested and imprisoned owing to his links to one of the conspirators. In the atmosphere of suspicion that followed, he was fined the enormous sum of £30,000. He was also committed to the Tower of London, where he was confined for 17 years. A month before the sentence was passed, the castle was leased to Sir Ralph Gray, the owner of nearby Chillingham Castle. Sir Ralph took no interest in the property and let the buildings deteriorate further. In response, and to ease his financial situation, the earl decided in 1608 to order the removal of lead from all the ruined buildings in the bailey.

In May 1617, James I and his court visited Warkworth Castle on their way to Scotland. The earl's officer, Captain Whitehead, wrote in a letter that the king did 'very much gaze upon it, only saying when he came to the tower where the lion is pictured on the wall: "This lion holds up the castle".' He also reported that some courtiers, who looked around the castle for over an hour, were angry to see it so poorly kept, with the buildings serving as shelter for sheep and goats and the park fence broken down. The earl remonstrated by letter with Sir Ralph over the despoliation of his castle, but to no effect.

When Sir Ralph Gray's lease expired, the great tower was being used for laying out oats, which had to be moved for the twice-yearly meetings of the manor court. In 1622, the castle was leased to Sir Francis Brandlyng, though what use he made of it is not known.

74

The Second Part of Henry the Fourth,
Containing his Death : and the Coronation
of King Henry the Fift.

Actus Primus. *Scœna Prima.*

Warkworth Castle

Below: Algernon Percy, tenth earl of
Northumberland, the owner of
Warkworth during the Civil War.
The portrait was painted by Sir
Anthony Van Dyck in 1636–8

THE CIVIL WAR AND ITS AFTERMATH

The history of the castle during the Civil War (1642–8) is
obscure. It was garrisoned for the king but surrendered to the
invading Scots in 1644. In 1648 the Parliamentarian forces
installed a garrison, and when the soldiers withdrew they
were instructed to remove doors and iron so that the castle
could not be held in war. It was later claimed that they had
demolished parts of the building. Possibly they reduced the
bailey to its present condition. In spring 1649, Algernon Percy,
tenth earl of Northumberland (1602–68), sought redress for
the damage, but nothing was forthcoming.

Amazingly, the great tower survived. Its reprieve was brief:
in 1672 the widow of Jocelyn Percy, the eleventh earl
(1644–70), gave its materials to one of her estate officers,
John Clarke, to build a new house. Offered half a crown for
every load of spoil, local labourers stripped 272 carts of
material from the condemned building. Just 26 years later,
however, one John Carter was instructed to estimate the cost
of restoring the great tower as a residence.

His recommendations – had they been carried out – would
have had a profound effect on the form of the building: all the
windows would have been replaced, many floor levels

changed and the whole structure re-castellated. The substantial cost of the work was estimated at £1,600, or about £900 if the necessary materials were stripped from the castle at Alnwick. Perhaps fortunately for both buildings, the work never took place and Warkworth gradually languished as a ruin.

THE REVIVAL OF WARKWORTH

For most of the next century, the castle was neglected. In about 1752, the wall between the Montagu Tower and the gatehouse was demolished and the stone used to build cottages. The Carrickfergus Tower also partially collapsed. But, even before the close of the 18th century, the buildings became an attraction for tourists, with interest increased by Bishop Percy's popular poem, *The Hermit of Warkworth*.

The Percys, by now elevated to the dukedom of Northumberland, began to take an active interest in the property. The demolished castle wall was rebuilt, probably in the late 18th century, and clearance of the site began, with substantial excavations in the 1850s and 1890s. As part of the 1850s work, the fourth duke, Algernon Percy (1792–1865), employed Anthony Salvin to restore the great tower.

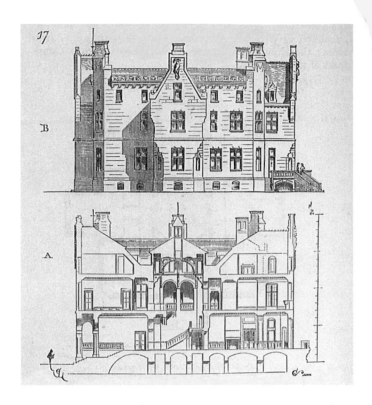

THE DUKE'S ROOMS

Preparation for Anthony Salvin's restoration began in 1849.
The intention was apparently to restore the whole building,
but the work done between 1853 and 1858 was more
limited. External stone was replaced where necessary, and
two upper chambers, known as the Duke's Rooms, were given
new floors and roofs. These rooms were used for picnics and
outings from Alnwick. In 1901, Eleanor, dowager duchess of
Northumberland, whose husband had commissioned the
work, recorded their furnishings. One room had a leather
wallpaper stamped in gold, purchased from the Mancini Palace
in Venice. The other was hung with a series of tapestries
bought in Rome. A craftsman in Saddleworth made a set
of furniture ornamented with Percy arms and mottos in a
late medieval style. He claimed that he had incorporated
fragments of furniture from another Percy castle, at Spofforth,
Yorkshire, but the pieces appear to be entirely Victorian. *The
Builder* (1860) reported that the rooms created, '... when the
ornamental carpets are unrolled, and the sideboards set out
with choice specimens of ancient ceramic art, a very cabinet
picture of an interior in "ye olden times"'.

Salvin's work probably brought the attention of the
19th-century French restorer Eugène-Emanuel Viollet-le-Duc
to Warkworth. He copied its plans to produce a model for
an ideal country house. Among the concessions he made to
modern living were the conversion of the hall into a drawing
room, the chapel into a saloon, and the buttery and pantry
into a billiard room.

*Above: Elevation and section of a
model country house, designed by
the 19th-century French architect
Viollet-le-Duc, who based it on the
great tower at Warkworth*

*Facing page, above: Dorothy Ann
Scott, wife of Jim Scott, standing in a
doorway at Warkworth*
*Facing page, below: Jim Scott,
caretaker of Warkworth in the early
20th century, in the gatehouse of
the castle, with his horse and barrel
for collecting water*

Memories of Warkworth

Dorothy Thompson recalls her family's connections with the castle:

'My great-grandfather Jim Scott was the first caretaker in our family at the castle, in the early 1900s. He would, I think, pay rent to the duke because he kept his animals there. But Mum would leave a bowl at the gate for visitors' tuppences. They'd have to have some remuneration, wouldn't they?

'It was hard work. Auntie Nancy said they were up at six o'clock scrubbing the steps of the entrance. There was no water and my great-grandfather would go to one of the breweries in the town with the horse and this old barrel on wheels to fill it up. This water must have been for washing as well, unless they went to the river and had a dip.

'They kept rooms clean specially for the duke. And when the duke and duchess brought visitors from Alnwick for the day, my great-granny made tea for them because it was a great event.

'Great-grandfather was feared by the kids: he'd say, "Quaa doun off those walls!" – he was Scottish – and they'd scarper.

'There were three boatmen who took people up to the hermitage – one of them was my Uncle Jim. Mum said that, as a girl, she almost drowned at the landing. There's a deep hole there and when she was landing the boat, she slipped and fell in. Fortunately, there was a doctor on the boat, and he saved her life.

'We always had spectacular pageants at the castle. They'd re-enact the history of the Percys, climbing down a rope from the first-floor window of the keep – it was very daring. And we used to have carnivals on the river, with all the boats and the banks of the hermitage lit up. Mum used to win prizes for the best-decorated boat.'

'We used to have carnivals on the river with the boats and the hermitage lit up'

Above: The castle in the course of
clearance in the 1920s. The chimney
stack of the custodian's former
lodging built into the gatehouse is
clearly visible

THE CASTLE AS HISTORIC MONUMENT

At the turn of the 20th century a caretaker and his family
lived in the castle gatehouse. The caretaker paid rent to the
duke for grazing his sheep and ponies in and around the
castle. The roofed Duke's Rooms in the great tower were
maintained for the use of the duke and duchess of
Northumberland, who would bring guests from Alnwick
Castle for picnics in the summer and made regular visits to
the town and the estate farms. The castle and hermitage were
also a holiday attraction for visitors from Newcastle and
villages in the area, and an annual flower show, sheep dog
trials, historical pageants and carnivals were held there.

In 1915, the castle was declared a scheduled ancient
monument, and in 1922 was taken into state guardianship,
although the Duke's Rooms remained under the control of
the Percy family. Two years later, the moat was re-excavated
and the road up to the castle constructed as a means of
relieving unemployment. The custodian was also moved out of
the gatehouse, which was described by one official as 'entirely
unsuitable for a dwelling house', and the building was
conserved as a ruin. At least two further attempts were made
to roof the rest of the great tower, the first at the suggestion
of the scholar W D Simpson in 1938. Both were rejected on
practical and conservation grounds. The Ministry of Works
did, however, approve an application to use the great tower
as an air-raid shelter in 1940. The castle and hermitage came
into the care of English Heritage in 1984, and the Duke's
Rooms in 1987.